Sonia
Zosimo

THE CODE ENFORCEMENT SURVIVOR HANDBOOK

Some Basic Information to Help You Survive a Career in Code Enforcement

SANDRA MOORE

Bloomington, IN  Milton Keynes, UK

authorHOUSE®

AuthorHouse™
1663 Liberty Drive, Suite 200
Bloomington, IN 47403
www.authorhouse.com
Phone: 1-800-839-8640

AuthorHouse™ *UK Ltd.*
500 Avebury Boulevard
Central Milton Keynes, MK9 2BE
www.authorhouse.co.uk
Phone: 08001974150

First published by AuthorHouse 7/10/2007

ISBN: 978-1-4259-6234-0 (sc)

Library of Congress Control Number: 2006908099

Printed in the United States of America
Bloomington, Indiana

This book is printed on acid-free paper.

Forward

Why I wrote this book

When I first decided to write a book about code enforcement, I discovered that few books have been written about this subject. There have been numerous articles written about it, but not much beyond the usual newspaper or magazine clipping. It then occurred to me that as long as I have been working in this field, that it's possible I might have something to say about it. I actually have considered writing about code enforcement for a while now, perhaps the last three years or so, but this consideration didn't just pop into my mind on its own. It was a suggestion given to me by a couple of my co-workers who told me that I should definitely write about it one day. But to be honest with you, I really didn't believe there would be any interest out there for this type of book. Usually, people want to read about more engaging or heroic occupations such as that of a police investigator or a firefighter. In my opinion, not a lot of people would believe that an occupation that is involved in the investigation of code violations could be very interesting; if anything, they would probably think that it sounds pretty dull. However, as I mention in Part I of this book, there seems to be a growing interest in this type of work as evidenced by the job increases in the code enforcement field. But somehow I find it hard to believe that a person would wake up one day and remark, "I want to be a code enforcement officer one day when I grow up!" It's a little difficult to understand why a normal person would choose to work in the code enforcement field. Code enforcement is one of the most frenzied types of jobs in the working world. It's chaotic, unpredictable and unsafe. You can receive a fairly decent paycheck in this line of work, but if you evaluate the amount of verbal abuse one has to take and the potential for even physical abuse in this line of work for the amount of money you are paid, you will realize that on some days it really doesn't pay enough. Of course, there are a lot of days where it does pay to work in code enforcement. The job can be easy enough as long as things are going well, that is, when you can get a lot of cooperation from people and are able to resolve problems with relative ease and close some of your cases. And, there can be satisfaction in situations where you really are helping people, which, believe it or not, is not uncommon in this field. Not only that, but you will realize that you are a strong component in an organization that is instrumental in improving the general quality of life in the city or county where you are employed.

It must be stated that the examples used in the chapters of this book are not based on any actual occurrences in my employment, or others in their employment with other cities or counties. If there is a mention of a particular situation it is done merely as a characterization of what can happen in the field of code enforcement. Nothing written in these chapters represents any specific event, or is a reference to any specific individual or group of individuals.

My hope is that this handbook will give you some insight into what code enforcement is really like to help you decide if it's right for you. Unless you know someone who works in code enforcement and can tell you some interesting stories, I don't believe you would really grasp what it's all about on your own. That is my purpose for writing this book. Whether you decide to choose a career in this field will ultimately be up to you.

Introduction

What is code enforcement anyway? Code enforcement put simply is the investigation of code violations. Codes and ordinances are adopted by a jurisdiction and are enforced by a particular department or agency, as specified in the chapter of the local ordinance that designates who will have authorization to carry out the enforcement duties. Fire inspectors and building inspectors inspect buildings also for code violations, but their investigations usually pertain to a more specialized type of code investigation. For instance, building inspectors primarily focus on new construction, that is, construction that has not been completed yet, but that which is being proposed to be completed sometime in the future. They will also look at building safety, for the purpose of determining if a building is structurally sound, or for disaster-related investigations, for example, after an earthquake, fire, accident or natural disaster. Fire inspectors or fire prevention specialists as they are often called, will investigate buildings after a fire has happened to determine the cause of the fire and they will also check buildings and properties to ensure they comply with fire-safety requirements to prevent a fire from occurring in the future. A code enforcement division or department is an agency that is involved in the investigation of all different types of building and land use laws. The codes range from various zoning, building, municipal, housing, dangerous building to other miscellaneous codes and ordinances about everything from illegal encroachments in the public right of way to violations of a noise ordinance. The investigations are initiated usually by a complaint that has been registered to the department by a citizen or other source. If it is a building or zoning issue, it is almost always about a construction or a land use issue that has occurred after-the-fact. In other words, if it is about construction, the alleged violation is about something that has already been completed and is being used illegally and contrary to code. If it is about a land use issue (zoning), then it is usually related to a use of property that is contrary to the allowed use for that particular piece of land or structure. And then there are the local ordinances which are also adopted by the jurisdiction such as a property maintenance code, which contains code sections related to the condition of the property, for example, junk cars, trash and debris, weeds, graffiti, etc. Enforcement officers or compliance officers are employed by the city or county to enforce the various codes and ordinances described above. They compile research consisting of property records and information, permit records, and other important files and documents pertaining to the property, such as planning development files and public hearing cases. They write notices to property owners and all other interested parties of a particular parcel of land, and issue citations and prepare cases to go to the city attorney or county prosecutor in the event there is non-compliance. Code enforcement officers sometimes have to work early evening hours or on weekends to find specific violations that tend to occur only after normal business hours.

Code enforcement personnel are employed in a majority of the larger cities and counties in the U.S. and a career in this field is fast becoming an attractive occupation to both men and women in this country. It can be a dangerous occupation too, depending on the level of crime and housing problems in a particular city. It is interesting that until very recently, there were few women who sought careers as building inspectors or fire prevention specialists. This is now beginning to change. A lot of women have become code enforcement officers in the past ten years or so; many of them start out as code enforcement officers and then move into a career in fire prevention or building inspection. All of these occupations are related in that they are directly involved in the enforcement of codes and ordinances that regulate land and building use, and were written with the intent to protect buildings and their occupants from safety hazards. The only difference is that the manner of enforcement and duties of the enforcement personnel may vary from city to city and between counties as well, depending on the type of enforcement policy in place in a particular jurisdiction. In some jurisdictions, code enforcement officers require little education, usually just a high school diploma to qualify for a position, but do require some law enforcement background or familiarity with construction or laws pertaining to construction inspection. However, these minimum entry requirements are beginning to change, due to the complexity of new laws and changing roles of the enforcement officers over the years. Code enforcement officers in most cities and counties receive ongoing training and education, due to this need to keep up with new codes and ordinances relating to land and building use.

Contents

PART I

The Evolution of Code Enforcement

1

The history of code enforcement - how it all began

Imagine a city over one hundred years old. It has likely changed considerably throughout the years, to the extent that if you were to look at old photographs of it when it first became incorporated into a city, you probably wouldn't even recognize it. And over the years, the city's growth would lead to substantial changes in the demographics in relation to median income levels, housing units, ethnicity and population. You are also thinking that while growth can always be a good thing in that it brings commerce and jobs to a city, it will inevitably lead to some sort of urban decay in the long run. And of course, you would be right. If you're like some people, you would tell yourself, "When it gets too big and my neighborhood begins to fall apart, I'll just move!" And that's ok. But what if you are unable to move, or just don't want to leave? Perhaps you grew up in that city and feel attached to it. In that case, you might have wanted to do something that would have helped

3

improve your city's appearance by getting more involved in neighborhood preservation activities. It was this type of thinking that eventually led to citizen action that caused cities everywhere to begin looking at the revitalization of run-down neighborhoods and preventing them from forming in the first place. Hence, code enforcement was born.

The enforcement of codes and ordinances has really been in existence in many cities for a long time. For the most part, it has been around in some form since around the 1960's to 1970's. However, it wasn't necessarily labeled as 'code enforcement', nor were there individual city departments that dealt with it at the time. Instead, most jurisdictions handled code enforcement complaints through a simple review process in their building or planning departments. If they felt it was serious enough of a problem to investigate it, they would give it to a building inspector or perhaps a police officer in some cases. For example, your neighbor's annoying rooster could have been handled with you taking the matter in your own hands by going to your neighbor and telling him to get rid of it or it would be shot and end up on someone's dinner plate! Or, you might have called the police, but perhaps all they could have done was to tell the person to find a way to take care of the problem or they would be given a ticket for disturbing the peace. If you were lucky enough and there was an ordinance prohibiting roosters in the city limits, someone from the planning or building department would have possibly taken your complaint. It was not until the late 1970's or early 1980's, and only in a small number of cities in the U.S., that certain kinds of code enforcement programs were finally being developed.

Early code enforcement complaints involved the investigation of a limited number of land use and building violations, but later, as the many different types of code complaints increased and were brought to the attention of city officials, code complaints involved a much broader spectrum of code violations to be considered, such as property maintenance, noise, and abandoned vehicle abatement. And of course, as the elected officials of these cities noticed that it only made sense to have a code enforcement program in their community, the number of code enforcement complaints grew as the citizens realized they could request the assistance of their city leaders to help them resolve problems within their neighborhoods.

By the mid to late 1980's however, the cities that had a code enforcement program needed to hire more people to handle the ever-increasing complaints. Thus, 'code enforcement officers' or 'code compliance officers' as they are now often called, were employed. At this time, it was usually only seen in the larger cities, particularly along the western and eastern coast cities in the nation. The general attitude of most small towns during this era was that code enforcement wasn't necessary, perhaps due to the fact that most of these cities and towns had small populations, therefore, they didn't have a lot of blight-related problems. Perhaps these cities found the whole concept of enforcement to be a waste of time and they rebelled against bringing more city government in with 'big brother' watching them. Even where code enforcement programs did get their start, many people were resistant to the idea of more laws being enforced by the code police or, if you were a code enforcement officer during this time, you may have even been called the 'Gestapo' or a 'Code Nazi'! But one thing people did begin to realize as they noticed that code enforcement was working so well in other cities, there seemed to be a direct correlation between code enforcement cases and crime statistics. When neighborhoods became blighted, crime increased, and therefore, in order to keep crime levels down in their communities, they needed to begin looking at code enforcement in a different way.

Thus, the idea of code enforcement became more and more popular, and the city leaders wanted to have it, so they began setting aside more money to put into their cities' budgets for their individual code enforcement programs. Many of the code enforcement budgets have increased dramatically since the late 1980's. You can see this by taking a look at the number of code enforcement officers cities have on their payroll compared to how many they had back then. And, as the number of code enforcement officers increased, so did the number of clerical support positions, which increased the code enforcement budgets further. If you are looking at code enforcement as a career, it is obvious that it is one of the fastest growing fields in the country, one that is just now beginning to get everyone's attention.

So now you might be thinking, "Why should I care about the history of code enforcement, and why is it important to know, if I choose a career as a code enforcement officer?" It is important to know why and how code enforcement got started simply because as a code enforcement officer you would be serving a very important purpose in your community. The purpose of code enforcement can be seen in most cities' mission statements. A lot of these statements talk about improving the quality of life in the city, or something similar to this. What better way is there to improve the quality of life, than to be a part of an organization that helps improve the city's appearance by removing blight and deterioration? It is all part of conserving and safeguarding that which is good about a city and removing that which is bad. Therefore, if you choose a career in this field, know that while you will be dealing with a lot of unique and difficult situations, you will be fulfilling that particular city's historical promise of initiating a code enforcement program and expanding it over the years, in order to preserve the city's good aspects, so that the community can enjoy it at its best.

2

Why code enforcement is here to stay

Now that the city leaders and politicians decided they wanted a code enforcement program for their city, it wouldn't be going away anytime soon. If you look at the cities across the country that have had a successful enforcement program and talk with the people there, you will find that code enforcement has had a significant impact on their city in general. More often than not, those cities have improved greatly in their overall appearance. So why would any city or county do away with it? It has happened before for sure, but those cities or counties that for whatever reason, got rid of their code enforcement departments paid a very dear price for it. When something like this happens, not only are jobs lost, but the effect on the municipality's appearance begins to rear its ugly head everywhere throughout the community. However, now the complaints still come in on a regular basis, but someone in another department will have to handle it. And, no doubt that someone is already overworked and unable to deal with the problem promptly or effectively. What you end up with is blight and decay in a lot of the neighborhoods where the good people move out and the bad ones move in. As mentioned before, blight leads to an increase in crime. Where you see graffiti and trashy yards you usually see criminal activity. Sadly, they go hand in hand and this in turn burdens the police force as well. Most police departments today have some sort of police problem-solving unit that educates the public about forming a neighborhood watch program and similar task force groups. But the problems are solved much more effectively where code enforcement is used in conjunction with these programs. Police departments everywhere normally would fight to keep code enforcement around. Fortunately, the voice of many police agencies is strong and most politicians bend favorably toward helping the police manage their jobs better, therefore, are more than happy to give them what they need, which would include a viable code enforcement program. In addition, if the city were to try to remove a working code enforcement program, they would most definitely hear from all the citizen activist groups which would be fully formed and in operation by then. These groups are notorious for being quite vocal in their communities and demand that code enforcement is there for them at any given time. These citizen activist groups are usually comprised of neighborhood watch foremen, police volunteers, code enforcement volunteers, and neighborhood association board members who regularly attend city council meetings and local neighborhood improvement meetings. Most cities have their fair share of them and they are not going to disappear into thin air. These types of activists will not stand by and quietly watch while their city does away with a code enforcement program. There would be an army of them showing up at city hall for a protest! And these are just the neighborhood groups that are concerned with the residential communities. In most cities, you will also have active business groups and leaders who are taken very seriously by the city leaders because they bring revenue to the city and are part of an influential network that is capable of encouraging other businesses to move into the city. Most businesses won't move into a blighted town. Why? If they do so, they risk losing their investment because most people, if they had a preference, do not want to go to businesses in run-down areas. Also, the owner of a business wouldn't want to risk starting a business where a lot of crime exists, that is, to be an open invitation to theft or vandalism. So it is apparent that all of these neighborhood associations and business groups desire a safe and clean community, and although they are dedicated people and work very hard on neighborhood preservation, they can't do it alone. They must have help and support from the city leaders and a good, working relationship with the city's code enforcement department and police department. As you drive through the neighborhoods and business districts of your city, try to imagine what it would be like if no one cared about it. The kind of people who usually don't care about their city's appearance are the criminal types, and as mentioned before, these types are the ones who will move into the blighted regions, forcing the decent people out. This is why code enforcement is here to stay and will remain in existence forever.

3

The future of an ever-changing profession

In most jurisdictions where code enforcement first got its start, the programs dealt mainly with housing, building and zoning violations. These types of complaints actually do cover a long list of enforcement possibilities. However, over the years, the code enforcement agencies became a sort of 'catch-all' division where complaints of many different varieties were investigated. If the complaint was unique or unusual, it always found its way to the code enforcement department. There's a good reason for this. No one else wanted it! So, in addition to handling the usual complaints regarding an illegal garage conversion or business out of a residence, today, a compliance officer might receive a complaint about someone draining their swimming pool into the street, without first de-chlorinating the water. Or, perhaps they'd receive one about the gentleman next door to an elderly woman, whose motion light shines directly into her bedroom window at night, thus preventing her from sleeping for the past five nights. The latter two types of complaints mentioned above may have been routinely dismissed back in the early 1980's. But code enforcement officers today must be prepared to investigate a wide range of complaints. There are two main explanations for this. As cities become more and more customer-service oriented, they seldom refuse to take a complaint, unless it would be one that is deemed a civil matter. In such cases where there is no municipal or state ordinance on the books to give the agency the authority to enforce it, the complainant (person registering the complaint) may choose to pursue the matter in a civil court of law. Also, new laws and ordinances are continuously being enacted that must be enforced by a particular agency. The responsibility for enforcement almost always ends up falling into the lap of the code enforcement department for a city or county. And, along side the increased responsibilities of code enforcement officers is the widened scope of the officers' general powers and duties. A lot of code enforcement departments have issued uniforms to their officers and some even carry defense weapons, such as firearms! Still, other code enforcement officers have the power to perform an arrest on an individual, perhaps with or without a defense weapon. You can see from this that code enforcement evolved into more of a division of a police department in some jurisdictions, rather than a division of a planning or building department. The trend today seems to indicate that code enforcement is becoming more of a professional field, one that requires more experience and education than ever before. Most entry level code enforcement positions require only a high school diploma and some minimal law enforcement or construction inspection experience to qualify for an open position. However, as the competition gets tougher due to the increased interest in code enforcement jobs and the recognition that it takes an intelligent and resourceful individual to work complex code enforcement cases, jurisdictions everywhere are beginning to emphasize more and more the importance of education as a major deciding factor in the hiring process. There are many classes available now in construction inspection as well as courses in general law enforcement. And of course, experience can always be helpful, but many first-time code enforcement officers have zero experience in code enforcement work, but make up for it by being experienced in some other law-related field. The bottom line is that if you are going for a code enforcement position, you're better off if you have a two year degree as opposed to only a high school diploma, or are certified in code enforcement or building inspection rather than only having taken a couple of law enforcement classes. Code enforcement is by far becoming one of the fastest growing career trends in the U.S. This is one profession that didn't even exist forty years ago. But today, the number of code enforcement officers or code compliance officers keeps climbing higher every year. One day soon, there could be as many as twenty officers for a city of 50,000, depending on that city's budget. This is partly due to the fact that the position of a code enforcement officer is becoming much more specialized. For example, some cities and counties will hire an officer who handles only those complaints regarding abandoned vehicles or perhaps illegal businesses. Gone are the days where the officer works cases involving only some zoning and building issues. There are numerous new ordinances being adopted by the cities, which always generate more complaints that need to be investigated. In addition, there are specific code problems that require weekend enforcement, such as the illegal businesses that only operate after normal working hours, primarily because these people are well aware that most cities have limited staffing on weekends. And, there are also more violations of the sign ordinances occurring over the weekend as well, such as real estate, garage sale, and special event sales of one form or another. Hence, many cities hire part time officers or flex-time officers who can adjust their schedules to cover these days and times when a special type of enforcement is needed. You can see that as the needs of a particular city change over the years and there are new trends that arise in a community, the realm of enforcement expands and requires the hiring of additional staffing and training to meet those needs. A good example of this can be seen with what has happened with garage sales over the years. It used to be that having a garage sale was a simple process of putting out some household items you no longer wanted in front of your house for sale. You probably advertised in your local newspaper prior to the sale, and by word of mouth via your neighbors and friends, who helped make your garage sale a successful one. Around twelve to fifteen years or so ago, the normal garage sale evolved into a major sales event in some cities. People were plastering signs all over fences and utility poles throughout the neighborhood and as far as several blocks away. And, for some reason these same people disrespected the community by not removing these signs after the garage sale was over. These signs were left up for days afterward, while they wilted in the sun and eventually blew off and littered the streets and sidewalks. People who lived in apartment complexes wanted to jump on this bandwagon too, and began having multiple sales along several street blocks with these same types of cheap cardboard signs illegally posted everywhere imaginable. Cities everywhere were experiencing this growing problem. These garage sales began to look more like mini swap meets within the residential districts and needless to say, concerned citizens began to complain rather loudly to their city council members. Eventually, new garage sale and sign ordinances were adopted and the cities could now limit the number of garage sales and restrict the signage to a bare minimum. But obviously it doesn't just stop here. Even though this particular problem was addressed and brought under some control, you can bet new predicaments will emerge as societies evolve over the years. It is then when the city officials will have to work together to come up with new solutions to deal with these unique kinds of problems.

Another interesting change is that as municipalities try to lean more toward education, they find themselves changing job titles and department names as well. Some cities don't like the word enforcement, so they use compliance instead. For example, the title, 'code enforcement officer' is instead, 'code compliance officer' in many cities.

You will also begin seeing some new and innovative ways that code enforcement will use in order to expedite complaints and streamline case work. It is highly probable that in the future, code officers will be using lap top computers in their official vehicles and writing notices to people in the field the majority of the time, to cut down on excess time and expenses related to generating notices from the office. Many cities and counties have already begun doing this. It will always be necessary to investigate code violations, it is how and to what extent that will matter the most in the future.

PART II

Investigation Basics

4

The complaint process

Let's say that you were the favorable one they selected for the code enforcement officer position you applied for. Now what? You are about to receive your first assignment, your very first code enforcement case. In most cities the process happens something like this. A citizen will either phone in or submit a written complaint form. Some cities are now referring to this form as a 'request for investigation.' Then, the clerical staff receives it and logs it in an entry log book and/or computer system data base. A hard file is many times created so the officer can use it for keeping a written chronological log and for maintaining copies of important documents such as notices and memos. Once all the preliminary information is entered and recorded where necessary, the case file is given to the code officer, in this case, you. You must first review the complaint by reading through the written complaint, which in some cases is challenging by itself! Sometimes the handwriting is so sloppy it's illegible or the sentence structure leaves a lot to be desired. After you decipher the complaint, the next step is to compile any additional information to help you work the case. For instance, if you need to look up any planning file information, county assessor records, or building permit records, it will be necessary to obtain them prior to writing an official notice to the property owner, tenants, business owner, property manager, etc. It may be one or a combination of the above, in other words, whoever has legal interest in the property. After you compile the necessary preliminary information and documents and make copies for your hard file, you will perform the inspection of the property. In some jurisdictions, a courtesy type of letter may be mailed to all interested parties where applicable, before the inspection is conducted. This way, the person is notified ahead of time that a complaint was filed against their property, which can many times prompt the person to take care of the problem before you get there. When you are finally able to perform the inspection, you must lawfully identify yourself when entering onto the property, and explain why you are there to whoever is in charge of the property when you arrive, in order to gain entry onto the property. One instance where this is not necessary is in the situation where there is an imminent danger to the public or the occupants of the property. If you see exposed electrical wiring strewn across a wet driveway where children may have access to it and the wiring extends to a dilapidated shed being occupied for living purposes, this may be one such example of imminent danger. Also, you should make a reasonable attempt to contact someone on the property first, and then you would clearly have the authority to enter onto the property in order to determine what action should next be taken to abate the code violation. However, in the majority of code enforcement cases, the situations do not rise to this level of seriousness. In every inspection, where the officer has to enter onto the property, the officer must first identify themselves in the accepted manner and get consent from a person in control of the property at the time, prior to performing the inspection. In most cases, these inspections are not thwarted. Nine times out of ten, people will allow you to enter onto their property, but sometimes you must use a lot of persuasion, though you will get better and better at this with experience. Some inspections are done without going onto the property, so there would be no need to identify yourself. You will then observe the areas you are able to access for violations of any codes and ordinances and take any photographs, if necessary, for further documentation. If you observe no violations, the case can be closed. If violations are observed and noted, then the next step would be to write the official notice as mentioned previously. In most jurisdictions, ten to fifteen days is the usual prescribed time period in which a person must comply by removing the violation(s). After this time period expires, a pre-citation notice may be sent, that is, if this is the policy for a particular jurisdiction, or the officer can go straight to writing a citation to the person in violation. Depending on where you work, a citation can be administrative or criminal, or both. An administrative citation is basically a civil citation that is handled through a collection process whereby it can end up in civil court, if it goes that far. In the case where a criminal citation is issued, the offender must appear in court, usually within thirty days to plead their case. And ultimately, if this person still refuses to comply, the case can be forwarded to the city attorney for prosecution. And, if it does go that far, you are basically done with the investigation portion of this case, unless your city attorney requests additional information or inspections, or if you will be required to testify as a witness in a court of law. However, you would not be able to close the case until the problem gets resolved, but it will now be up to your city attorney to compel the violator to comply, instead of you. Many of the cases you will be working won't make it to your city attorney's office. This is because people usually comply long before then, perhaps with a little 'persuasion' from you. I will discuss this persuasion factor in a little more detail in the next chapter.

Most code enforcement cases are resolved within ten days to three months, but some can take as long as two to three years. This would be the norm for a building code violation or a complicated zoning issue. An example of this type of case could be a person who takes their time in getting all their required inspections, sometimes for a good reason, such as, lack of money to finish the project. And every city has its own history of cases that have taken several years to resolve, some as long as five years or longer! In such cases, the original officer who worked the case at the beginning may not even be employed with that city by the time the case gets closed. Once a case is closed it is most likely filed away in a cabinet, and after so many years, the hard files may be purged and sent to a records center where they can be stored on a CD disk or microfiche. Otherwise, imagine how clogged up a file center would become after hundreds of these cases over the years!

A code enforcement officer feels satisfaction every time a case is worked through to the end and successfully closed. It is an enormous relief when a case you've had for several years that measures around two inches in thickness, is finally resolved and removed from your desk! An officer must learn patience and endurance in order to work cases such as this from the beginning to the end.

5

Profile of the typical enforcement officer

This occupation seems to attract former law enforcement officers or people who have had some type of law enforcement background, although this is not always the case. It seems many retired police officers, highway patrol officers, security guards or jail guards are looking for some type of law enforcement-related work, minus the everyday stress and dangerous working conditions. Frequently, when they get hired on to become code enforcement officers, they find that some of that same stress they left in their previous careers is found in their new careers as code enforcement officers. The only problem is, in most cities, code enforcement officers do not carry defense weapons, so they may feel a sense of uneasiness when adjusting to this new kind of work. And then there are those who have had some type of construction-related background, such as permit clerks or construction inspectors who are familiar with the building and housing codes. It is possible they are looking for more challenging and interesting work and will find that in this field. Now let's look at the general personality traits needed in order to be the typical code enforcement officer. For starters, it takes someone with guts! Add to this, patience, a good sense of humor, empathy, and common-sense judgment. Without these necessary traits, it is doubtful you will survive in the sometimes unpredictable and frenetic world of code enforcement. Additionally, if you tend to have a weak stomach or a soft heart, you'll struggle every day in this line of work. It has been said many times by many experienced code compliance officers that this is definitely a job where you will wear many different hats. During the course of your career you may play the role of a psychiatrist, a referee, a parent, a philosopher, an educator, a police officer, a social worker, an actor, and a diplomat, to name a few. Consider this scenario. You receive a complaint about a man who lives in a house that is filled almost to the ceiling with piles of trash, old newspapers and magazines, food wrappers, discarded junk, etc. And the yard doesn't appear much better. This person is someone well known in the code enforcement realm. He's a classic case of a pack rat. In fact, the condition is sometimes referred to as 'pack rat syndrome' or 'hoarder's syndrome'. So what type of personality can handle such a person? Perhaps it would be someone with a lot of empathy. How about patience? And now, you the code enforcement officer who gets this complaint must choose a role to play in order to be as successful as possible, because you may be dealing with a person who has some emotional problems or phobias. Also, you might need to enlist some help from other agencies by acting as the middle-man. In the first instance, you might be role-playing as a psychiatrist, in the second, a social worker. Do you think this sort of switching between roles is an easy task for a rooky code enforcement officer? It most likely is not. Perhaps a retired police officer would have an easier time with it. But for most, experience that comes from working hundreds of code cases is essential in helping a code enforcement officer learn how to handle such difficult people.

Throughout your career as an enforcement officer expect that you will deal with all kinds of people; their dispositions will range from angry to apathetic, disagreeable to somewhat agreeable, normal to neurotic, and even-tempered to emotional. You will have to learn the art of persuasion, which can get tricky at times, but it is a necessary element in getting people to comply. When you constantly have to switch from all these different roles, you are actually performing this art. Let's try another scenario. You receive a complaint and respond to someone who is regularly dismantling vehicles in his driveway. You pull up in front of his house in your city or county vehicle, and there he is, pulling an engine out of a truck which is parked in the driveway and up on wood blocks. You then identify yourself and explain why you're there. At first, this self-professed mechanic is accepting and seems willing to comply. But in just a few minutes he is beginning to appear agitated. It obviously needed some time to sink in. Now Mr. Mechanic changes gears on you (no pun intended) and begins to proclaim his rights as an American. How dare you come onto his property when it is a free country, and tell him what he can and cannot do on his own property! Ok, it's time to grab a couple of hats. Put on your educator hat and quickly switch to the police officer one. Because now you will need to explain to him the zoning laws related to residential property while at the same time you will need to keep him calmed down enough to understand it. Good luck! The typical code enforcement officer has to be capable of guiding a person into compliance with the codes, knowing which hats to put on and knowing what type of personality they're dealing with at the same time. If they come on too forceful, he or she could cause the most easy-going person to become a tyrant, thus completely defeating the purpose. Let's face it; we're all capable of becoming obnoxious ourselves, if pushed far enough. You will need to learn how to 'persuade' not 'dissuade' people to obtain the results you would like.

The typical code officer must learn to fine tune all these skills in order to successfully work their cases. If you are unable to do this, you will suffer endlessly from a backlog of cases that don't get resolved in a timely manner, which leads to stress, then burnout.

6

Case management and problem-solving

To prevent burnout that can easily happen to a person working too many cases, one of the first things you will need to learn how to do is manage your caseload and resolve the various issues as efficiently as possible. Too many times an officer will get caught up in the middle of matters that will bog them down in a mire of useless spent time and energy.

I strongly believe that any caseload that exceeds sixty in number is far too many. Once you are carrying a caseload larger than that, it becomes more and more difficult to work the cases efficiently. And especially this is true if you have several cases involving complex building and zoning issues. These types of cases usually require a lot more time and paperwork, much more so than the simpler property maintenance cases. What typically occurs when you are laden with too many cases is that there is a high likelihood that some important ones may fall through the cracks and get lost or forgotten. This can be dangerous because if something bad happens as a result of it, or a citizen calls and questions why nothing is being done on a case, you will be asked to provide justification for your lack of action. But if you're fortunate enough to work for a city or county that has enough code enforcement officers to balance the workload, you will have a much easier time managing. It is important for you to set goals and prioritize your workload, so that you can keep your caseload down to a minimum. Let's say one week you receive five cases about trash and debris, three cases regarding building additions or alterations without a permit, and one stating someone is living in a house without water or electricity. Which one of these should receive top priority? Which one of these can be inspected later, perhaps the following week? These are the decisions you will be making initially as you weed through your inbox and choose how to prioritize your cases. In case you're wondering, the complaint regarding a house being occupied without the required utilities will obviously receive the first priority. Depending on what it was that was constructed without a permit, you will probably decide which of those three building code violation complaints should be looked at first. Obviously, if the construction deviates far from minimum building code requirements and is alleged to be unsafe, this would take priority over the others.

And there are other ways in which you can learn to manage and streamline your caseload, especially when you are carrying a large one, such as, one to two hundred cases or more. You will have no other choice but to learn creative ways in which you can lighten your load. Sometimes these methods can be so simple, that code enforcement officers are oblivious to it. For example, I find that I can zip through a lot more inspections if I go out in the field during the morning hours as opposed to going out in the afternoon. It is true that in most areas traffic tends to be much worse in the afternoon, making traveling time from one location to another almost twice as long. In addition, most schools dismiss schoolchildren in the middle of the afternoon, further contributing to traffic congestion. Of course, there are times when you must set up some of your inspections later in the day to accommodate the public. But in a large majority of the instances, you should be able to schedule many of your inspections earlier in the day. Also, as difficult as this can be at times, try to keep distractions in the office at a minimum. The more employees who are hired in a code enforcement division in closer working spaces, there seems to be a lot more noise and annoying little distractions in an office setting. It is so important that you don't allow these distractions to slow you down in working your cases. It is extremely difficult to write complex legal notices when people are standing around work stations gabbing endlessly about personal matters. Don't misunderstand me. In this line of work, we need a little diversion now and again and socializing with your co-workers can go a long way in helping you get through a stressful day. A good joke or a little office levity can actually improve employee morale, and there have been many articles written about that subject. This is not what I am referring to. I am referring to the people who stand around talking for more than ten minutes at a time about everything under the sun that has nothing at all to do with work. You may have to learn some ways in which you can work in the office and avoid these disruptions. You might consider wearing earplugs or going to another work station that is quiet and away from the noisier sections of the office.

It's one thing to find ways to streamline your workload, become more organized, and set goals by prioritizing your caseload. Now comes the hard part. In the last chapter, I talked a lot about what it's like dealing with people and their special personality traits. Before you perform an inspection, you most likely will not know who you are going to be dealing with, even if you have had a chance to talk with them initially over the telephone. This is because many times people don't always begin to show their true colors until you meet them on their own turf. In other words, when they meet you in person on their property during your initial inspection, they may decide now that reality has set in, they don't like hearing what you're telling them, and at that point become antagonistic. So, you always want to make sure you're ready for this sort of attitude change.

Solving problems can be a simple process or a complex one, depending on the circumstances of your case. I'll use an example to illustrate this. Suppose you receive a complaint regarding an older, dilapidated house that is owned by an elderly woman who lives with her daughter who is a drug addict. You are informed ahead of time that the daughter controls everything including her mother, and finances her drug habit with her mom's social security checks. The mother is afraid of her own daughter and does nothing about it. When you arrive to perform your inspection you also see there's a large amount of junk, trash and debris surrounding the house. When you attempt to gain entry after you identify yourself, the daughter becomes irate and tells you to get lost, denying the inspection. At that point, you would have no other choice but to leave the property. You could consider an inspection warrant, but don't be too anxious to pursue one yet, because it may not be necessary. I have worked for a city for several years, and although the possibility that a warrant could be necessary popped up a few times, I never had to obtain one. Let's go back to the problem. We know we have some type of elder abuse taking place, because the mother never sees her money. And there are plenty of code violations on the property, which further indicates that the money is being spent on something else. You will probably want to contact a social worker from an elder abuse center in your community. Also, you will want to inform your police department so they can accompany you on the next inspection or do a separate investigation on the drug activity there. These are actions that can start the ball rolling even though you aren't able to gain access onto the property yet. Also, the more people involved in your case, the more witnesses you have in the event it ever goes to court. You may also want to try to contact some family members such as any other children, if any exist and live locally. There is always the possibility that children do live nearby, but are not even aware that a parent is being abused by one of their own siblings. You read about these kinds of sad stories in the news all the time. In the illustrated case mentioned here, you may have to approach this passive mother when the daughter isn't home, and in this case, she would be the legal owner of the property anyway. Once you are able to get through to the mother and gain access onto the property, the problems can hopefully begin to get resolved.

So there you have it. These are the types of situations in which you will learn how to manage and prioritize your caseload, evaluate what type of personalities you are dealing with ahead of time, plan a course of action to take, and then take action to resolve the problem. Case management and problem-solving is what you will be doing over and over again as a code compliance inspector. It is imperative that you learn how to do this early on if you want to survive.

7

Letter of the law vs. spirit of the law

When code enforcement officers first get hired on they are sometimes like others in law enforcement where they tend to come on a little strong and heavy-handed in the beginning. As I mentioned before, if you push people too hard, they may become aggravated, which will hinder your progress in working a case. There is an old saying and it often applies to code enforcement, "you can catch more bees with honey"! This does not mean to say that you must sweet talk everyone you encounter in the field. There is a time and place for it, however. And many times, after initially evaluating the situation, you will find that when you look at the overall picture, it isn't always necessary to enforce the codes at all times to the strict letter of the law. This also does not mean to say that you will ignore the law. There are many ordinances on the books that may not be ignored or twisted in any way. This particularly pertains to many of the building and housing codes, and many of the zoning ordinances, too. But sometimes when working a property maintenance case you will find that you need to "see the big picture" and focus on the portion of the complaint that really matters. Suppose you receive a complaint regarding an elderly man who has neglected his yard over the years due to his physical condition as well as his financial situation. When you perform your inspection you see a lot of junk in the front and rear yards, as well as an inoperative tractor in the rear yard. And let's just say for the purpose of this example, that the written complaint only mentions the junk and debris, and after you speak to the complainant, they are not concerned in the least about the tractor, even though there are cobwebs growing around it and it's surrounded by a chain-link fence in the backyard, so it is clearly visible from the neighbors' properties, too. The gentleman who owns the property is very cooperative but tells you that in no way is he able to comply within the ten day period of time, because he can't afford the dumping fees all at once. But he gives you his word that it will be cleaned up in the next thirty days. Also, he tells you that he really wants to keep his tractor, if just for sentimental reasons. He then tells you that he once proposed to his late wife on the thing! If you were to enforce the code violations on this property to the letter of the law, you might tell him that while you sympathize with his sentimental feelings, the law is the law, and the tractor has to go. And, although you may compromise and give him one additional week to take care of the problem, there is no way he's getting a month! On the other hand, if you decide to enforce the codes to the spirit of the law, you might review the complaint and see that the complainant was only interested in the piles of junk and debris on the property and could care less about the tractor. So why pursue it? After all, it's parked in the back yard and the only people who can see it are the two or three neighbors adjacent to him. Unless they come forward with a written complaint addressing the tractor, there may be no immediate reason to pursue it at the time. You may also agree to the thirty-day time frame, as long as the gentleman agrees to allow you to do progress inspections where you might come back to the property in ten or fifteen days, then again a week or so after that, to make sure he's working on the problem.

Also, realize that you must really make an effort to evaluate the situation and see the big picture as I mentioned before, because you may be put in a situation where you will have to justify your actions. But if you have documented your findings well and are able to stand by your opinion, you should not run into difficulty in these circumstances. Let's say for instance you receive a case regarding a room addition that was alleged to be constructed without a building permit. Once you have completed your research, you find the necessary building permit records that show that the addition was authorized and constructed under a permit issued more than forty years ago; however, there was never a final inspection. Nonetheless, your research does show that there was an approved framing inspection. If you were to follow the absolute letter of the law in this case, you would require that a final inspection be obtained on the permit. Your determination would be based on the section of the building code, which requires that all buildings must have a final inspection prior to use and occupancy. But on the other hand, if you were to follow the spirit of the law, you would decide not to require final inspection. Your determination would be based on the facts that show the construction passed the framing inspection, which is basically one of the last required inspections anyway, just prior to the final inspection. The proposed construction had already been approved and obtained all the required inspections under the codes that were in effect at the time of construction. You could look at the age of the construction and determine that the building has been in existence for a very long time and has stood the test of time. Unless there is an alleged safety hazard, it may be pointless to pursue it. As a code enforcement officer, you must possess the ability to see the "forest for the trees," as the famous expression states, repeatedly throughout your career as these cases find their way to your desk.

These are simply illustrations of what happens when you decide to enforce a particular code violation using the spirit of the law rather than the letter of the law. Circumstances will arise several times in your career where you will need to make use of your common-sense judgment along with a combination of your knowledge and logical reasoning skills.

Every city or county has its distinct written and unwritten policies as well. Some jurisdictions will advise you up front during the interviewing process where they stand on enforcement. You should try to adopt the attitude that it's not always a good idea to see everything in black and white when enforcing the law, and remember that there are some gray areas where you have to decide whether you should use the spirit of the law vs. the letter of the law when working a particular code case.

8

Be safe out there!

It is only fair to warn you that code enforcement can be a very dangerous occupation at times. This is where your survival skills will be needed the most. One such survival skill is the gift of intuition. If you don't possess this natural ability then you may one day find yourself in trouble. I feel pretty fortunate that I have such an intuitive knack. It has helped me in countless ways, especially when working in the code enforcement field. It is especially useful for people, like me, who tend to be a little too trusting and naïve at times. But when that sixth sense or intuition kicks into play, and it seems to every time I have needed it, I know when it's there and how to listen to it. Sometimes, I can walk up to a house and that feeling enters my mind, and believe it or not, I can feel it in my body too. I really can't explain it to you any better than that. Quite honestly, I have always felt a sense of intuition at times, but it gradually became a stronger sense the longer I worked in code enforcement. And even if you think you don't possess this ability right now, give it time. I believe that over time and with a little experience, you will begin to develop these intuitive skills, too. Police officers have developed this ability as well, but I don't think they necessarily possessed it when they were fresh out of the academy. Call it whatever you want, survival instinct and a result of their training in defense tactics, but I'm sure they will tell you that they were not aware of it when they started out as rooky police officers, but the longer they remain in their careers, they become aware that they must listen to their intuition. It also seems as though women tend to have this gift more so than men, for some reason. Perhaps this has to do with the fact that as women, we were always conditioned to be more in tune with our feelings and emotions, so we learned early on how to pay attention to them. When that intuition tells you that you need to leave a property, then you need to listen to it and do exactly that. There's absolutely no constructive reason for hanging around when you sense danger. It will not cause your case to get closed any sooner, and it will not mean that you are a coward or are avoiding work. It is for exactly the opposite reason, that you will achieve your purpose in the end, but stay uninjured or alive!

But what happens if you do find yourself in a dangerous predicament where your safety could be compromised? It is possible you may have to rely on some self-defense techniques you've learned, or, if your city or county has issued their officers with pepper spray or other self-defense gear, you may be put in a position at that time to use them. But, in a lot of cases you will probably be able to talk your way out of the bad scenario or just disengage and leave the area. How would you know when it's that time? Suppose you are talking to an owner of a property who is in violation of one of the building codes, and as you are telling him what he needs to do in order to correct the violation, he begins to walk closer and closer to you, all the while staring right at you while his complexion becomes dark red and his veins begin to protrude in his neck. Although no two scenarios are alike, there are times when you will be able to talk to a person and get them to calm down. But if you can see it will not work with an individual or group of individuals, then that would be the moment in time to disengage and leave the scene. Or, if the person has stepped too close to you and is inside your space and appearing to be a direct physical threat, then you would obviously have no choice but to defend yourself according to your city or county's specific policies regarding self-defense when reasonable.

Another big safety concern for code enforcement officers are the canine encounters. It's even worse for code officers than it is for postal carriers, who also have to be on the alert for this danger. Code enforcement officers have to physically enter onto a property and sometimes go into a rear yard to inspect areas behind the homes, and frequently, a dog will be in that back yard. If you've been reading the news lately, the problem with out-of-control dogs has increased substantially over the past few years. The hostile dog issue has always been a menace to code officers, but it has developed into a more serious problem in recent years as the problem with drug traffic has increased; drug dealers notoriously keep guard dogs on their properties to alert them when someone is coming to their homes. Also, irresponsible dog breeding is on the rise, and as more people are obtaining the more violent breeds, it has grown into a serious problem all over this country. New legislation is now being enacted to counteract this problem, but as always with trying to put new laws into place, it takes a long time to get these laws on the books. In the meantime, you will at least need to carry pepper spray on you or have a police officer accompany you when you suspect there may be a vicious dog on the property. And don't take for granted that just because a dog might look friendly, that you will be safe from aggression. So always be ready, and do whatever it takes to ensure protection from canine attacks.

In the best-case scenario, prior to your inspection appointment is a better time to decide whether you will need police assistance, but you will not always be able to coordinate with the police ahead of time. Do not ever feel that you are bothering the police department or sheriff's office by contacting them by radio when you need a back up. Law enforcement officers are usually more than happy to assist code enforcement whenever possible, simply because they like to help us. Basically they want to scratch our backs and we want to scratch theirs. As long as I can remember, police and code enforcement enjoy the cooperative effort from both departments because so much gets accomplished when both are working together on a specific problem. If you do run into problems in the field or have an intuitive sense that you are about to encounter a problem, you should not hesitate to call for assistance from the police or sheriff's office. Keep in mind though not to get in the habit of contacting the police every single time you go in the field. In a lot of instances it really isn't necessary to have police assistance at every one of your field inspections, and the problem with relying too heavily on police support is that you will never develop that intuitive capability I have been describing in this chapter. Once you become better at using your intuition, you will automatically know when police help will be needed.

In a lot of your housing inspections, you could expose yourself to potential health and safety hazards, and this is due in large part to the very nature of what you will discover during a typical wide-ranging housing inspection where numerous violations are found. These are the inspections where a code enforcement officer can sustain injury or contract an illness if precautions are not taken. For example, if there is exposed electrical wiring or disrupted asbestos, a gas leak, raw sewage or a heavy infestation of cockroaches in a building, you have to be very careful not to touch anything or get too close to those affected areas. Gloves and/or masks are worn nowadays by a lot of code enforcement officers to protect themselves from disease or other air-borne hazards.

And be very, very careful and aware of methamphetamine laboratory locations in your city or county. Properties where drug manufacturing occurs are extremely dangerous to code enforcement officers and police officers because they are notoriously booby-trapped with makeshift explosives, hazardous electrical wiring and vicious guard dogs. A hazardous materials team should be on site with you during your inspection and you should also be equipped with full-body protective gear. Bear in mind, you want to be able to go home at the end of the day, so train yourself to be ready for anything that can happen.

In order to protect yourself in this line of work you must rely on your intuition, recognize the time to either leave the scene or defend yourself, know when police back up will be necessary, and be prepared to protect yourself from all the recognized hazards. That is, if you want to survive. Remember, be safe out there!

PART III

*The Effective Code Enforcement
Program - The 3 T's*

9

Team work

You have probably heard this term so much now, that it sounds like all the other professional buzz words of today. There are a lot of clichés such as "team playing" and "team building" being used in the business world today and unfortunately, some have played out their usefulness. However, it appears that team work is one such cliché that has stuck around for a very good reason. I believe that team work is a very essential element in your division's organization in order for your department to be successful as a whole and for you to be successful as a code enforcement officer.

The best way to talk about team work or team playing is to begin by defining it. This is a simple definition I have created for a practical characterization of team work in a professional setting: A team is a group of people who are the workers in an organization who are managed by one or more people who are the managers or supervisors of the organization. The management people are basically the coaches for the team and the workers are the players on the team. The entire group, which includes all the "coaches" and the "players" is known as the "team." When everyone in the group is working together, the entire group is doing what is known as, "team playing" and the result of this is "team work." When one or more workers in the group refuses to work with the rest of the workers, then the entire group is not playing as a team. It is important to understand that it is the entire group working together professionally and resourcefully that supports the organization and helps it to run as efficiently as possible, as a team.

You might be asking yourself now, "How does this relate to code enforcement? After all, don't most code enforcement officers work their own cases independently of one another?" The answer is yes and no. While as a code compliance officer you will be working a number of cases solely by yourself, there will sometimes be occasions where you will need to seek advice from co-workers, and perhaps even their help in assisting you in inspections. I'll give you some examples of this. Suppose you are aware that a co-worker has more knowledge than you on a particular zoning issue because they have had more experience with it. You might want to ask them for their advice or ask them to review the complaint for some insight into problem-solving the case. Also, sometimes it helps if two code enforcement officers perform an inspection together, especially in a case where you have prior knowledge that the people who reside on the property may be less than cooperative. Or, perhaps the other officer can speak a foreign language and can help interpret for you. Another example of team playing would be in the situation of a code enforcement sweep. Occasional proactive sweeps are done in some cities where inspections are performed proactively to enforce code violations in certain targeted neighborhoods. Officers usually work in groups of two or three officers at a time. Often one group will finish the sweep before another gets done, so they will contact them via radio or cell phone to see if they need any assistance. This ensures that some officers are not working longer on the sweep than others, and that the number of cases generated is fairly even between the officers. So you can see from these examples I listed that team work is extremely important in code enforcement. Not only is it essential in the office setting, but it is equally, if not more so, important in the field, especially with this type of work.

Team work does not mean to say that every single person is always working with every member of the team all the time. This is not realistic. Often, scheduling conflicts and other last-minute situations will arise, preventing the entire team from being able to work together at one time. But as long as there are enough officers to work a particular detail in the field, then that would be sufficient to accomplish what you set out to do. And teamwork effort is equally important between departments and divisions in your city or county as well. If the various departments are not working together as a team, then this will result in a breakdown in communication, which will defectively interfere with your code enforcement program.

We all have our good days and our bad days. You will definitely need the support of your fellow code enforcement officers and your supervisors with this type of work, because code enforcement in general can be a thankless job. Of course, I did mention previously that you will have some rewarding experiences too, so don't let that discourage you. Keep in mind that in order to help make your job easier you will want to work constructively with everyone. Remember, what goes around comes around, and if you support your co-workers, including all clerical and technical workers, they will eagerly offer you support, too. This is what team work is all about.

10

Training is a must

Do you know of any job in the private sector where the employer does not train its people well?   If you do, I'll bet there aren't too many of them.   In the private sector it is crucial that companies properly train their workforce because they invest a lot of money hiring those employees. But unfortunately, there are still some cities and counties out there that may tighten the purse strings a bit when it comes to allocating money for education and training. This is not a good idea.   The bottom line is that if an organization has good people who are qualified to do the job, they should want to make sure they hold on to them and that they are worthy of being promoted.   If a city or county values the people they have hired, then they need to make sure they are constantly being trained in all areas where necessary.   This should apply to everyone in the division or department, not just the new hires.   There are many areas where education, training and improvement are indispensable. I cannot stress enough that education and training should be available to all employees in your department.

Training may be consisted of any of the following: It can be comprised of anything from attending a half or whole day seminar about dealing with people to a one-day class on a new computer program to a full semester course on the building codes. It can be a foreign language refresher course, a certified officer training class or a mini-seminar on management training. Training can run the gamut of all kinds of different classes and seminars in a range of categories. This is the norm for code enforcement. There are so many areas where improvement can be made as I mentioned before, because this is the kind of work that changes continuously over the years and requires updated information on a regular basis. While this is true of many other types of careers too, it seems it is especially evident in the code enforcement field, due to the number of new ordinances being adopted by the local governments and new laws being enacted every year.

Also don't make the mistake as some officers do, in that they believe that because they have worked as a code compliance officer for so many years, they really don't need any more training. I have to admit that I have been guilty of this belief. We all tend to become fairly complacent at times and comfortable where we are, so we don't wish to make the effort to pursue any more education. And sometimes our management people can get busy with other priorities that they don't realize you haven't had any additional training for a while. This is why it is really important that you let your supervisors know when you think a little training can be helpful to you. In other words, speak up! You will always need further education in code enforcement, and even though you might have the most seniority in your department, this does not mean you won't benefit from more training.

While this applies to code enforcement officers, it also applies to the management staff. They should also be receiving ongoing training. If your managers do not realize the importance of education and training even for themselves, it is doubtful they will put emphasis on regular training and education for their employees. In order to be as effective as possible working in code enforcement, you must be receiving ongoing training and education. Without the required skills and education, you won't be successful in this career and may find it a struggle to keep up and survive.

11

Trust - An important element in working with people

And now we come to the last of the three 3 'T's, which is trust. Trust is basically faith combined with a little bit of instinct and a lot of experience. It is something that happens when you feel completely confident when dealing with a person because you know they won't let you down. By now you can see that it's an absolute necessity when working code enforcement cases. You have to be able to trust the person you sent a notice to, that they will make the required corrections in a timely manner. You will need to be able to trust the complainant to provide you with accurate details. And, you will need to trust your citizen volunteers that you can rely on them, just as they have relied on you. Believe me, there will be many occasions where you won't be able to trust some people, because they may not tell you the whole truth. Some people do this because it is their inherent nature to do so. Others do it because they feel backed into a corner and do it out of fear or because they are hiding something. Regardless of the reason for it, you will need to be ready for it and know what to do. You may work a case where you may catch people in the act of doing extensive remodeling work or converting a garage. When you ask them if they obtained a permit prior to commencing the work as required per the building code, expect that you may not get all the answers at first. For this reason, it is very important that you win the trust of the people you work with both in the field and in your office because you will need their help and support in getting your cases resolved.

But how about being able to trust your management people? The job of code enforcement is difficult enough by itself, imagine what it would be like if you were not able to trust your supervisor in that he or she will back you up whenever it becomes necessary. If you have a supervisor or manager who will give you guidance when dealing with a complex matter, and will stand by you when you need their support, then you are truly fortunate. And, I absolutely believe that communication on both sides is extremely important, too. You have to feel you can trust your boss by being able to share your opinions and feelings with them on a particular matter. In turn, your boss must have enough faith in you that he or she respects your feelings and opinions on any given situation. Of course, this does not mean they should give in to you every time you come to them with a problem or concern, or just because you might be more knowledgeable about a particular issue. It just means that you should not have any reservations about coming to them with a specific problem or sharing your views with them. Because code enforcement is such a thankless occupation at times, it is critically important that you become an appreciated and respected employee in your division, and supervisors and managers must work on developing trust in their employees, thereby valuing them and believing in them.

But, if for some reason the trust isn't there now does not mean it can never be developed. It takes a lot of effort on both sides to build this kind of trust. If you feel you don't have your supervisor's trust now, then you may have to make some changes on your part, to allow it to grow. Hopefully, if your supervisors see that you are working on building trust with them, maybe it will set the foundation for them to do the same for you. Building this type of trust with everyone you deal with in code enforcement is vital for you to be able to work through your cases successfully. Without this trust, you will have trouble surviving in any work environment.

PART IV

Can you Survive this Job?

12

Surviving the test

You will test several times before getting the position of code enforcement officer, but the real test will occur after you are hired. Statistics show that if a rooky police officer can make it through at least five years in the department then there is a good chance they'll make it to retirement, if they don't get injured on the job. This is due to this thing called stress. It is interesting that the average time a code enforcement officer lasts in his or her position is around five years as well. Sometimes they will leave a particular city and go work for another city or county, believing the grass is greener on the other side. Sometimes they will transfer into a different department of the same city, in an entirely different line of work. Others will move into another area of law enforcement altogether. But throughout my years at the city I have worked for, I have observed that the average time in code enforcement by an officer seems to be anywhere from three to seven years. Code enforcement work is stressful, and it's an unusual kind of stress. Police officers and firefighters are given more respect than code enforcement officers to be sure. Even though police officers must endure an enormous amount of stress on a day-to-day basis, the general public looks up to them because they not only represent positions of authority, but they wear uniforms and weapons, and are trained to react quickly to defend and preserve life. In most cases, a police officer is welcomed by the citizens of a community because they give them a sense of feeling safe and secure. People who work for the fire department are rendered this same type of respect and admiration. Building inspectors enforce building codes too, like us, but the public asks them to come to their properties to perform inspections on new construction. But how does the general public view code enforcement officers? Although some citizens welcome you, especially the ones who register the complaints, not too many other people do. You are sometimes seen as a threat and are not welcome on someone's property. Though they may decide on their own to cooperate with you, they don't normally greet you with open arms. This common attitude from the public by itself can create stress. As a rooky code enforcement officer, if you want to remain in this field for awhile, you must prepare yourself to endure in this kind of environment.

Throughout your career expect that you will work cases that are complex, alarming, tragic and frustrating. Some of your cases will evoke emotion from you, such as anger and sadness, and you will have to fight back against allowing that to affect you as you are striving to be non-judgmental while trying to resolve the case. Remember when I talked about how you cannot have a weak stomach if you want to do code enforcement work? On occasion, you may receive a case that may cause you to feel some discomfort. Consider a case where a mentally ill woman is living in a dilapidated house, and there is animal feces throughout the interior and exterior of the property. Consider, for the purposes of this example, the woman has approximately fifty cats, in varying stages of poor health that are obviously being neglected. The outdoor cats are roaming the neighborhood and creating a nuisance for her neighbors, as they defecate in their yards and tear up their flower gardens. The indoor cats are urinating on the floors of the woman's home and the cat boxes are overloaded with clumps of fecal waste, and there are cat feces in every room of the house. Sounds like a handful doesn't it? Welcome to code enforcement. These are the cases that will try your patience and tug at your heart. And these are the cases that will test you time and again throughout your career.

In addition to these trying kinds of cases, you must learn to survive the test of handling a multitude of cases in various settings and circumstances. Even though there may be enough code compliance officers in your division, it always happens that people will be out sick or on vacation, and your staffing levels will be lower on any given day or on several consecutive days. The complaints will still need to be handled by someone, and the public isn't concerned who does it, as long as it gets done. You will also be tested by people in the field on a daily basis. The complainants will expect you to work a miracle by solving the problem in less than a week and the people in violation believe you're being too unreasonable, no matter how much time you give them. So, there is no way to win! It would be a miracle if you could make everyone happy at the same time, but this doesn't happen very often in code enforcement.

Regrettably, the people you work with may test you at times also. This is that unfortunate problem we call office politics that we must all learn to accept and work around. The only comment I have to say about office politics is that it takes on many forms from spiteful gossip to office cliques. These behaviors are harmful because they create resentment in the workplace. It has no place in a professional setting and it's up to your supervisor to nip such behavior in the bud. Though it is expected that your supervisor will test you now and then, the longer you stay in your position and gain more experience, over time, it should occur infrequently. When a supervisor constantly looks over the shoulder of a code enforcement officer, the officer will feel he or she is being micro-managed and it could hinder performance. In the end, this goes back to one of three T's we discussed previously, which is trust. If your supervisor or manager trusts that you are competent enough to do the job, there would be no call for micro-management. Once you pass your probation, you have pretty much proven you can work in code enforcement, it's how long you last afterwards that becomes the more important question.

13

Balancing politics; understanding priorities

Politics is everywhere. It's not just in certain cities or in high-level government. So, whether you work in the private sector or for a public agency, you might as well get accustomed to it. This is especially true in code enforcement, because code enforcement was basically produced by politics. It was the local governments, ruled by council people who were under pressure from all the citizen action groups that resulted in code enforcement programs being formed in the first place. For the purposes of this chapter, I am not going to focus on office politics. That's a subject all by itself, and that could take up several chapters. No matter what career you choose in life, you will have to learn to deal with the usual office politics. The politics I will be addressing here has to do with the local government politics that filters its way down to your division, and may have an indirect effect on your role as a code enforcement officer.

Periodically, you will have to learn how to prioritize your workload in the way that I described in chapter 6. Not only will you have to learn how to prioritize your cases dependent on the more serious complaints, but you will have to place some precedence on those cases and matters that have been designated as a priority by your supervisor or manager. You must learn to balance the workload by dealing with the more serious and potentially life-threatening code violations, while simultaneously attempting to satisfy a citizen who may have gone directly to a council member or the city manager's office, because they may be upset about a neighbor who has a large boat parked on his front yard that blocks the view of the mountains nearby. You've heard the old saying, "the squeaky wheel gets the grease!" This is what can happen at times in code enforcement, and you will have to learn how to work with it. Sometimes when it rains it pours, meaning you will receive four or five top priority cases involving health or safety violations along with these types of complaints. In this situation, the health and safety matters should take priority over the others. However, as soon as possible after addressing the serious housing or building code violations, you must take immediate action to deal with those other items.

It may be hard for you to understand at first, but your political leaders basically want the same thing you want as an enforcement officer. The reality is that everyone is striving for the same goal. It's just that the sensitivity to certain matters is sometimes different. Sometimes they do not understand how code enforcement operates and it will be up to your division head or manager to educate them. For example, sometimes they think code enforcement should be placing more priority on sign enforcement or that it should be more involved in proactive enforcement as opposed to reactive enforcement. Perhaps they believe more emphasis should be placed on cleaning up the business community. Whatever the case may be, you will benefit from seeing it from their perspective, just as they benefit from seeing it from yours. It is very constructive when council people get more involved and find out what code enforcement is all about and give it the support that is so necessary. In this way, the public sees that code enforcement in their neighborhood is an important aspect of the community and that the city or county leaders place a high priority on it.

Let's talk about political correctness. It exists in code enforcement like everywhere else in the government arena. It should be stressed that certain words or phrases need to be removed from your vocabulary. Although it would be very easy in this line of work to refer to a negligent property owner as a "slumlord", this is a term that could create some trouble for you, and why would you want the hassle of trying to explain your actions? You should also avoid other derogatory terms, such as "low-life", "dirt-bag", or "druggie". You get the idea, and I'm sure you will be able to find other ways to describe them.

Politics can become a little complicated when the press gets involved. Each jurisdiction has its own policy in dealing with reporters, so it is extremely important to be aware of this immediately, to avoid a bad situation where misinformation could find its way to the press, causing undue disapproval of your actions and embarrassment for you and your department. However, the press can be utilized to your department's advantage. There are many instances where positive events and occurrences take place with code enforcement, such as neighborhood clean up projects or a code enforcement sweep, where you can have a person who is designated to do a press release, inform your local newspaper to run an upbeat article about a specific constructive occasion being planned by your city.

Politics can be used to your advantage in a lot of cases, such as when it is there to support code enforcement in its many endeavors. It's unfortunate that politics has received so much negative publicity these days. No matter what city or county you will work for, you will run into political scenarios of one form or another. The end result of all this is that politics can be a very positive factor in code enforcement, as long as you and your supervisors understand how to make use of it so that it helps you meet your goals. Surviving politics is not difficult; it depends on how you react to it.

14

Thankless job or rewarding career

Code enforcement is probably one of the most under-appreciated jobs in the country. It is a job where you will receive few letters of commendation from the public. But expect to receive some angry phone calls and angry letters about you on occasion. Remember, you will be working in a field that deals primarily with complaints. You will be handling an array of neighborhood feud scenarios and tenant/landlord disputes where you will be wrestling to stay out of the middle in order to resolve the real issues. Don't get me wrong. You will be thanked on occasion and told by some members of the public that they appreciate what you are doing for them. Code enforcement is demanding work with endless deadlines and sometimes unreasonable expectations. It would be something similar to being locked in a room with thirty toddler-aged children! You can't please them all and they will continually demand your attention. There will be many times when you deserve commendation of one form or another and will get nothing, not even the simple two-word phrase, 'thank you' or even a nod of approval. Surviving this type of non-acceptance is trying at best. Think about all the service type jobs out there where the customer will thank you after you have provided them with good service. There are many. As a code enforcement officer in a professional organization, you will provide above average or even exceptional service most of the time. But you may sometimes feel that no one even noticed. This is because the public generally believes that it is your job to take care of the problem and you shouldn't expect anything in return. After all, they consider you to be a public servant, which implies you are expected to provide exceptional service while simultaneously solving the problem for them in a very short period of time. This is your duty, so why should they thank you, right? This attitude is now changing and people are becoming more appreciative of the role of code enforcement. But there are still times it can be considered a thankless job, for some very good reasons. Think about the conclusion of the average code enforcement case. The end result of a code enforcement action is that someone may be dissatisfied with the outcome. That someone, seven times out of ten, will be the one in violation. The others, in the three out of that ten, will be the ones registering the complaints. They will be unhappy because things didn't work out in the way they wanted, or they find out from you that no code violations existed and you are unable to resolve the problem for them. So you can always expect one party to be disappointed and vent their frustration onto you.

You may also feel at times that your own employer doesn't recognize you enough for your efforts. This is because code enforcement agencies are extremely busy departments with endless deadlines and priority situations. Your supervisor may be caught up in the middle of trying to rectify a bad situation where a citizen is complaining about a code enforcement officer's specific actions, or busy with some other damage-control agenda, along with all the other every day management affairs. For this reason, it would be tough for them to be aware of every single positive episode that occurred, or that you competently handled a particularly difficult case. So, not only do you feel unappreciated by the general public, but you may feel unnoticed by your own boss! Please do not misconstrue the point I'm making here. I'm not suggesting that you will rarely be thanked by your supervisor, or that the managers in your department will never recognize you for an achievement when recognition is due. But since there will be times in this line of work when they will miss something significant, it will seem as though your accomplishments are not being acknowledged at all. Also, because you will be receiving your fair share of negative feedback from people, it's human nature that as people we tend to concentrate more on the negative comments than on the few positive ones that filter in occasionally. You will experience a lot of negative encounters throughout your career so they will probably outnumber the positive experiences in this line of work.

But even though the job ranks fairly high on the list of the most thankless careers in the country, there will be moments that take place where you will find it all worthwhile. These are the rewarding experiences that pop up now and again; some of them are great accomplishments and some of them don't seem as significant by comparison. As hard as it is to understand for many, the job of code enforcement can be very rewarding at times. Take a look at the work being done out there. There are several blocks of neighborhoods being transformed! There are communities in some cities that used to look somewhat similar to inner-city ghettos before code enforcement came into play. It can take a long time, but these cities, with enough support from everyone involved, have made it a special project to change these neighborhoods back to what they were like years before, and have remained committed to keeping them that way. Is there a great deal of work and time involved in this undertaking? You bet there is! Just ask the people involved and all the people in those neighborhoods who couldn't afford to sell their homes and move. They will tell you that it was well worth all the time and money spent, the police involvement, and all the support from the citizen groups and city representatives. If you are lucky enough to see this kind of transformation happen in the city or county you work for, then you will definitely feel rewarded just in knowing you played a noteworthy part in whatever improvement was made, no matter how little your contribution was in the effort. It is a team working endeavor that involves the city leaders, the citizens of a community, the police, various other departments and code enforcement, and everyone has to give a little of their time and talents to make it a reality.

And then there are the smaller-scale accomplishments that will give you great satisfaction when everything works out well and according to plan. You will experience that personal satisfaction when you work a case where something very positive is the end result of your involvement in the resolution of that case. Let's say for example you were able to help an elderly gentleman find the resources he needed to get his property cleaned up, his roof repaired, or his fence replaced. This is definitely a situation that does not warrant strict enforcement to the letter of the law. If the gentleman does not have the money to make needed repairs or clean up his property, and you go all the way with enforcement, you and your jurisdiction would not only look foolish, but you may even anger a judge or jury if it ends up in court. But if you take the opposite approach in working a case such as this with the end result being that the violation gets corrected, both you and the elderly man will be satisfied with the outcome.

But, of course, you have to make a decision whether it's worth putting up with all the variable situations that exist working in the field of code enforcement. If you are willing to endure the everyday stress that comes from dealing with abusive individuals in the field and often-times angry customers in the office, then you may have the opportunity one day to experience the occasional rewards that do come to you. Before you are hired as a code enforcement officer or if you are just beginning your career, you might consider taking a seminar on assertiveness training, or a class on basic self-defense techniques. There are courses out there that are designed to teach you the skills on how to react to and work with difficult people and situations. Some of these skills you will have to learn through experience alone, but these courses can be helpful in that they will at least prepare you with some of the rudimentary skills needed in managing obnoxious people and challenging situations.

Code enforcement is a tough job that requires a determined person who is willing to work hard, and who possesses a high threshold for stress and a talent for dealing with intolerable people. If you can survive this type of working atmosphere, it will eventually bring you some of those rewards, you just need to have the patience to wait for it to happen.

Conclusion

Early on in my career, a gentleman I was assisting at the front counter in the building department told me I was much too charming to be a code enforcement officer when he met me for the first time. You might be surprised to learn this, but at the time I was insulted! All the while I thought I was giving the impression that I was a tough code enforcement officer and those people out there better do as I tell them, or else! Remember what I said in chapter 7 about the behavior of code enforcement officers in the beginning of their careers, how they tend to come on a little too strong and heavy-handed? I do not remember the exact details of that particular encounter because it was so long ago, but I do remember hearing that statement from him. And I do remember that I had been an officer for about a year or so, and was just beginning to discover that you can accomplish far more in code enforcement by using the golden rule in your approach to dealing with people. Needless to say in this particular case, the gentleman did everything I asked him to do, when I wanted it done, and I couldn't have asked for someone to be more cooperative than he was.

And, it's probably best not to expect the public to address you as 'Officer So-and-So' and wear a badge every time you go into the field. A softer approach would be to identify yourself by saying, "My name is So-and-So. I am a code enforcement officer for the City or County of Such and Such." Then, you could show them your ID card and hand them a business card. Your business card would state your name and job title anyway.

Most importantly, if you treat everyone out there the way you would like to be treated, even the obnoxious ones, and if you apply some of the suggestions I have mentioned in this handbook, you should be able to experience a successful and rewarding career in the code enforcement field. I realize there are some situations that are difficult to remedy. If you are working with a person who is mentally ill or someone who exhibits some other serious anti-social behavior, then you will need the assistance of others as I have mentioned before, in helping you work through those circumstances.

Whether you are at the beginning of your career, or are considering one in this field, my hope is that you stay in it long enough to appreciate all the work that you can achieve, by using your talents wherever and whenever beneficial. I believe that each person in a code enforcement organization has a special talent that can be used somewhere to really make a difference in his or her department. It may take you five years or longer to discover what that gift is, but you will never know unless you make a commitment to stay in code enforcement for a long time.

About the Author

Sandra Moore has worked for the City of Escondido since September 1988. She was promoted to a code enforcement officer in 1995 and has worked in the capacity of acting Senior Code Enforcement Officer and Business License Supervisor periodically since 2001. She has attended numerous training and education seminars in this field and is certified as a code enforcement officer through SCACEO (Southern California Association of Code Enforcement Officials), which has recently changed its name to the statewide organization known as CACEO (California Association of Code Enforcement Officers). She has worked literally thousands of code enforcement cases and her experience and knowledge in the field reveals itself through her common sense approach to dealing with difficult people and situations in the field as well as handling the day to day stress related to this type of work. She has attended several neighborhood group meetings and has given presentations to the various citizen activist organizations in the community. Her purpose for writing this book was to provide insight, along with general information and ideas to men and women interested in going into a career, or just beginning one in code enforcement. Her hope is that the stress and burn out that so often occurs in this type of job can develop itself into a more positive career learning experience.

15237262R00051

Made in the USA
San Bernardino, CA
21 September 2014